Burying the Mountain

Burying the Mountain
poems by Shangyang Fang

COPPER CANYON PRESS
PORT TOWNSEND, WASHINGTON

Cover art: Ye Cheng, *Mountain*

Copper Canyon Press is in residence at Fort Worden State Park in Port Townsend, Washington, under the auspices of Centrum. Centrum is a gathering place for artists and creative thinkers from around the world, students of all ages and backgrounds, and audiences seeking extraordinary cultural enrichment.

LIBRARY OF CONGRESS CATALOGING-IN-PUBLICATION DATA
Names: Fang, Shangyang, author.
Title: Burying the mountain / Shangyang Fang.
Description: Port Townsend, Washington : Copper Canyon Press, [2021] |
    Summary: "In Shangyang Fang's debut Burying the Mountain, saturated
    images of longing and loss rush through a portal of difficult beauty.
    Deeply immersed in the music of ancient Chinese poetry,
    Fang alloys political erasure, exile, remembrance, and death into a
    single brushstroke on the silk scroll, where our names are forgotten as
    paper boats on water"— Provided by publisher.
Identifiers: LCCN 2021025488 | ISBN 9781556596148 (paperback)
Subjects: LCGFT: Poetry.
Classification: LCC PS3606.A546 B84 2021 | DDC 811/.6—dc23
LC record available at https://lccn.loc.gov/2021025488

98765432 FIRST PRINTING

COPPER CANYON PRESS
Post Office Box 271
Port Townsend, Washington 98368

www.coppercanyonpress.org

For my grandparents

郑环琼 & 方清扬

For my teacher

Brigit Pegeen Kelly

花葉随天意，
江溪共石根。
早霞随類影，
寒水各依痕。

冬深, 杜甫

Contents

壹 I

5 Argument of Situations

7 Chronicles on Disappearance

8 Whether a Marble Confirms Its Feeling of the Field

9 If You Talk about Sadness, Fugue

12 Foretaste of Disaster

13 Almost Hour

14 Satyr's Flute

16 It Is Sad to See a Horse Sleeping

17 Celadon

18 Phantom Limb

20 Birthday

21 Aria of an Ebbing Scene

贰 II

25 Beethoven

26 Preludes, a Blue Plume

29 Incoherent Funeral March

30 Fish

32 Being and Time

33 Chaconne

35 *Easier to Lift a Stone Than to Say Your Name*

36 Calligraphy

38 Requiem

39 轰隆隆 Is the Sound of Thunder

41 Utterance of a Folding Fan

42 Through the Darkness

43 *Time the Stone Makes an Effort to Flower*

叁 III

47 Vermeer: Thief

48 A Difficult Apple

55 A Bulldozer's American Dream

56 Reliquary Evening

57 Meditation on an Authentic China

62 Red

63 What Sustains in This Autumn Rain

64 Comrade Mannequin

肆 IV

69 Serenade behind a Floating Stage

70 In the Movie Theater

72 Two Cannot

73 Thin Air

75 Lie Beyond

76 *La Traviata*

78 Tether

79 Nude Descending a Staircase

81 Training

82 The Boy Is Sleeping

83 Op. 64 in C♯

84 Acknowledgment: Erato,

87 Thanks for Reading

89 Displaced Distance as a Red Berry

93 *Acknowledgments*

95 *About the Author*

Burying the Mountain

壹 I

花	Blossom
葉	Leaf
隨	Abide
天	Heaven
意	Volition

Argument of Situations

I was thinking, while making love, *this is beautiful*—this

fine craftsmanship of his skin, the texture of wintry river.

I pinched him, three inches above his coccyx, so that he knew

I was still here, still in an argument with Fan Kuan's

inkwash painting where an old man, a white-gowned literatus,

dissolves into the landscape as a plastic bag into cloud.

The man walks in the mountains. *No, he walks on rivers.*

The man moves among shapes. *He travels through colors.*

The mountains are an addendum to his silvergrass sandals.

Wrong, his embroidered sleeves are streaklines of trees.

Neither could persuade the other, as my fingers counted

along his cervical spine, seven vertebrae that held up

a minute heaven in my hand. But it isn't important.

It is not, I said. It is just a man made of brushstrokes

moving in a crowd of brushstrokes. The man walks

inside himself. The string quartet of the tap water

streamed into a vase. My arms coursed around his waist.

We didn't buy any flowers for the vase. *It's okay.*

The sunlight would soon fabricate a bouquet of gladiolus.

To walk on a mountain for so long, he must desire

nothing. Nothing must be a difficult desire. Like the smell

of lemon, cut pear, its chiseled snow. The man

must be tired. *He might.* He might be lonely.

He must be. The coastline of his spine, the alpine

of his cheekbone—here was where we stopped—this

periphery of skin, this cold, palpable remoteness

I held. The dispute persisted. Are you tired? *I'm okay.*

That means you are tired. *You're bitter.*

Whatever you say. If my hands departed from his skin,

the heavens would collapse. The limit remained

even though we had used the same soap, same shampoo;

we smelled like the singularity of one cherry's bloom.

The vase stayed empty, the sky started to rain.

My toothbrush leaned against his.

The man must be lonely, I said. *No, the mountain*

is never lonely. Burying my forehead inside his shoulder

blades, the mountain is making itself a man.

Chronicles on Disappearance

There are seven sadnesses that don't belong
        to men. Seven cicadas make one motorcycle,

testing its engine in the dark. Everyone lugs
        their sorrow in their boots. Everyone

a half-open kitchen window, with souls sultry
        as boiled meat. Invalid are all objects,

closed to sorrow. Don't wake them up. Don't
        look, so that they let you (me) be your (my)

self. After all, our eyelids, another empress
        of a tyrannic dawn. In this country,

go to the grocery in the carcass of a pickup,
        return with carnivals. In another land,

the windshield wipers are lashes of a monk,
        lulling the world into one scarlet-dusted

reverie. On some evenings, above the Three
        Gorges cliffs, the monkeys fold their arms,

rocking gently in the rain. Identical to stones.

Whether a Marble Confirms Its Feeling of the Field

A marble is placed at the center of a field.
The marble does not speak for the field.
The field speaks for itself, senescent throat of a night wolf.

:

If the field were a deity, then the marble
would be an attentive immolation to which the field returns.

:

Phenomenologically central position
is what some call it when the marble is replaced with a you
& you, an axis, around which fabrics of awareness
undulate, coordinate.

:

In any case that marble is the godhead of the field
& the field no more than a dank, voluptuous, verdant dress
the marble attires, outspreading the river's blue stitchery.

:

Wherever the marble moves, the field follows.
Branches of elderberries throttle into corpuscles of senses.

:

Some would say the marble is the field's heart.
Some say it is a buck-naked song. Some insist
it's a blind eye feeding on the projection of your sight.
If they were right, the marble must be wrong.

:

If the marble is wrong, you must walk across the field,
while the others sit beside the marble & apologize.
Though the best of us keep walking without noticing the marble,
let alone the men weeping & the field burning in their grief.

If You Talk about Sadness, Fugue

1

Paul Celan wasn't necessarily the saddest person
in history. Trakl could have been sadder, though his sadness was personal.
The personal is unbearable.

2

I returned to China in the summer and found
summer didn't belong there.

3

The loneliest music is Brahms's First Piano Concerto. My friend said,
It's like drinking a bowl of Chinese herbs
in the dark.

4

Schubert is nonexistence.

5

Trakl wrote, *Your body is a hyacinth.*
And Celan drank milk when the night came.

6

This morning a boy in Syria, five years old, was rescued
from the dust. He wiped his head and saw the blood, didn't cry.
In front of the television, people wiped their faces draining with tears.
They didn't bleed.

7

In June, I bought a book of Silver Age poets: Akhmatova was the moon
of Russian poetry. Pushkin, the sun.

8

A girl, again in Syria, cried and raised her hands to surrender
when a journalist took a photo of her. She thought the camera was a gun.

9

I cried when I listened to Brahms. The dead became retongued.

10

In August, my aunt drove two hours to my town, begged me
not to be a poet. She read the poetry under my pillow and found out
Akhmatova's son was arrested. Gumilyov killed. Tsvetaeva went mad.
Everyone else exiled.

11

My aunt said, *We are still in a communist country.*
I told her, *I am already exiled by my family.*

12

The moon remembers; she witnesses in the dark.
I ask her to explain how we have forgotten to start with forgiveness.

13

For that boy, the war never ends. He shall not be lonely.
He shall repeat that motion of wiping, of digging his mother
out of dust, out of war-memory, brushing her hair stained with blood.
He doesn't remember his mother's name; he kisses her face.

14

Schubert had the body of a hyacinth. He wilted so fast.
Trakl added, *The last gold of expired stars.*

15

Celan's mother died in the war; he wrote poems for her.
He wrote, *It's falling, mother, snow in the Ukraine.*
Ukraine is the name of a place. His mother's name is *mother.*

16

I stopped writing poems, as my aunt had pleaded. I took the book back.

17

I close my eyes and touch the book as if blind,
to feel how cold each word is on the page, how sharp, like shattered glass.
I am afraid no one can keep it from falling apart.

18

The personal is unbearable. Someday, the moon will fall apart
from her memories. All night, she stared at the fleeting water, then left.
Nothing remained except
this calm stare of the ceaseless water.

Foretaste of Disaster

Young, therefore vain & wingless, he lets
his father tie a blue thread around his chest.
It is before the famous tragedy, the fall. Before
the imminent sea. The coast still composed
in subdued hues & regimented patterns.
The abstraction of waves has yet to be mutilated
by a scream. Human position yet to be tested.
He, at his prime, Anthony van Dyck, blazing
like an overripe Flemish peach, presented
this self-portrait, in which an old man tethers
a wing to a young man's pale, well-knit back.
Here, grief has yet to become visible,
as in Brueghel's—stick out of the water, legs white
as boiled chicken. In his early twenties, Icarus,
the trespasser or cross-dresser, was punished
for his pride. In his early twenties, Van Dyck
portrayed himself as Icarus in a painting,
in front of which I stand, looking him in the eyes.
Tomorrow, I will be a quarter of a century old.
My father disappeared like an antelope
into the dawning gold. But if & when Icarus
survives his drowning, stepping out of the sea,
as if out of a Cavafy poem, dripping
with synonyms of passion & desire, who
will untie the blue thread from his chest? Who
will save me? Come to change my life?

Almost Hour

Late night, but not too late for the father
to smash the plates. For his wife, made visible
by her nakedness. Sleepless is the neighbor boy
lighting a cigarette. It is now the half-lit hour,
hour of almostness. A cyclist passes by,
crushes the roadside lilies to spilled milk.
The streets are made marigold, damped
with lamps. The world is suddenly autumn.
Like a stranger in a long lost photograph,
I stand the correct distance from the present.

Satyr's Flute

I was skinning a goat's penis to prepare
         the dish my mother had taught me.
This was not in a dream, though, with a dream's
         deliciousness, the knife—a stroke of blueness
—tapered the bleeding thing into a sheer bruise.
         One must always be careful with a penis.
One must marinate it in a pool of oyster sauce
         with starch, sprinkle ginger juice to cleanse
its urinous smell—smell of fish—*ithyphallic,*
         as Rimbaud may have said—let the residue
of semen ferment with blood and the blueness
         into an evening sky like this: when the penis
starts weeping ceaselessly, softly at first,
         like a newborn, then louder, until the kitchen
turns into a train station, from which the goat
         was brought to the nearest butchery.
The penis cries like a baby, like a baby it cries
         for its wanting—without the mind
the penis is innocent. The penis wants
         its goat back. The way a child wants
his mother's milk. And the goat,
         without its penis, is it anyway
a goat? Half-male? Will it go crazy looking
         at the moon? Will it serve the Goat King
like a eunuch in a primeval dynasty?
         Or it will follow the rancid smell of dead
fish, past the meadow, past the bullying woods,
         to reach the lampblack river
and watch the water flow. Watch the needles
         of fish sewing the stream and wish
one of them was its genital. The penis in my hand
         is thick and emblematic, something I cannot
fully fathom. A device without the service
         of its mind, how does that work?

How, in heaven's name, can a mind bear to lose a part
            of its form and stomach the loss as a thought?
The thought of a penis, being nothing otherwise,
            is not a penis. How my mother once saw
me with a boy. How she said, *no*. The *n* preceding
            the choir of the *o* is like a castration
that severed me from her. O, am I anyway the penis
            my mother once lost? I rushed
back to my room, stayed a whole afternoon
            in front of the mirror and thought I am not
beautiful, thought she was right, no, I cannot
            love this boy in front of me. And wished
he had not been born. Now I can see how the goat,
            disturbed by his forbidden thought, staggers
toward that river, mates with deliquescent
            nymphs—Hermes into Hermaphroditus,
whose lilac-encased body, androgynous
            and gorgeous, once drowned
and rose from the rootless water. And I see
            the meadow outside the kitchen
is purple, an infecting pool of neutering
            tincture. The penis, enveloped inside
my hands, is old and tired, like a fetus curling
            back toward an anonymous uterus.

It Is Sad to See a Horse Sleeping

A horse is not a horse
when it's not running.
If a grasshopper could be a horse.
If a bruised boy.
I can't remember how I found myself
inside this story. Have I appeared too late
in the scheme. Too late to save anything.
Already, it's evening. The grass shines
its invisible green. The meadow
an emerald pulsing in a breast pocket.
Now, the horse a windmill in the field.
The mountains behind it, insurmountable.
Say it's the last horse in the world.
Say a bruised flower scents better
than those intact. Or I can still save
the horse & in saving the horse I will save
myself. But the horse has trained itself well
with terrible horselessness. The horse
is a broken fruit, a sweetness
no one can relish. *Wake up, Broken Fruit.*
I shake him. The horse isn't responding.
I lift his neck, strap his belly
like a scarf on my shoulders
& carry the horse
till my spine aches when a stem of aster
breaks. Ten thousand miles away.

Celadon

Watermarked like little maps, hands arrive
        with lamps. Wrists churn the river, erase

a mountain from the water's scarred surface.
        Only a boy's hand could perceive

such precision of tenderness. In his mind,
        the boy sculpts a dream being:

another boy, too beautiful, not like a boy at all.
        What is it like: a boy dreaming

of another boy's body? Must it be deadly?
        The evening is falling; the rain

grazes the horses' chestnut skin as they turn
        aimlessly among the birches,

their tense bodies lashed to the deep
        disappearance. And the magpies

kept awake by the stars. All night, their eyes
        brighten with indifference.

The boy walks among them, beside
        the quiet river, into the blue columns

of moon. The river flows cold and fixed.
        Suddenly, I rely on nothing to live.

Phantom Limb

after Hans Christian Andersen's "The Steadfast Tin Soldier"

The truth is, let's say, that the tin soldier did not fall in love
with the paper-doll ballerina. He fell in love with his missing limb.
Let's hold love in suspension. In a fictive afternoon like this,
the world is almost what it seems—*outside stood small trees around*
a little mirror that was meant to look like a lake. Honesty is this winter,
stripped bare. The mailboys quell their blue wings. The written deer
steps beyond the written water. Evident thirst. Evident is the missing
limb of this poem—the very world it ventures to transform
isn't there. There, for example, in an evening, Tadzio at the edge
of a sea, *divided from his companions by proud caprice,* like a lone god,
an apprentice of indifference, severing the water with his feet.
His hair flares into threads of sunset. He is practicing tragedy,
which in ancient Greek means *goat-song.* Tragedy is that a goat
doesn't sing. While its luxurious torso dissolves upon the machinery
of our tongues—Tadzio is, so to speak, conceptually handsome
and theoretically detached from this lush world, where the fleshy petals
in dawn cold and nectarines in June gold don't belong to any of us.
But how can one blame those who hold such a belief—perhaps
in springtime when the absent space is replaced with azaleas
tossing their enormous, ropy genitals—that the concept of being
soft in this world of firmness is at last possible. What it is isn't entirely
what it seems—the missing limb, at last, is the thing we always
carry inside us. That the nothing we lug without knowing, heavier
than anything, is at last our everything. The tin soldier fell in love
with his missing limb, Mann with his Tadzio, whose nonexistence,
whose evanescent-effeminate entity made of the very effervescence
of seawater, whose sleek skin cut of glass, form a silhouette like a kernel
of an almond, more bitter than Paul Celan's *Spätwort:* late-word.
The purity of language enters when words no longer resemble their
things. *Make me bitter. Count me among the almonds.* What's remarkable
about Celan is that instead of searching—in his last poems—he
becomes the missing limb. Words shatter like dropped fruits as he exits

this almost world while a well of wounded water closes behind him.
The moon will rise soon. Not too soon to make a vision, but soon enough
it perches in our imagination. So it may not be a bad idea to open
the window, pour a quarter glass of wine, finish the Mediterranean salad
and ambrosia for want of fried chicken, and think—*We were Danes
in Denmark all day long.* Think—salad, from *salata* in Latin: salty.
Thirst is the salt is a metonym of desire, in its severed past—*de sidere*—
from the star. Perhaps that is how all tragedies should have ended.
Perhaps this poem should have started with Stevens, whose lines
are twilight flossing pines, a practice of pantomime. Not to pretend
in hand there is a blossom, but to forget there isn't one. When the salad
is finished, the waste plate glares against the stark, nocturnal table
as a porcelain moon, a gallery of nakedness, emaciated as any self-
portrait. The plate makes an effort to resemble something, like a word,
except the something it resembles isn't there. Has never been there.
About his disfigured soldier, Andersen wrote, not despite, but
with his missing limb, he is the one who turned out to be remarkable.

Birthday

With permission, I return to Cavafy, whose verses
        reaffirm that love is not a euphemism

for lust. That shapely, firm flesh of youths
        is brazed in meters, their once lissome limbs

stirred by rhymes. I am not fooled by this illusion.
        Not again. Awake and alone in this world,

which entices my heart with images, then disciplines it
        with narratives, I finally recognize

that my life, consigned to the cursory flexure
        of a descending cherry blossom, is but a figure

with diminishment as its memory. Damage
        beyond measure caused by reprised imageries:

grasshopper, peaches, summer, formless faces—
        desire reconstructed as destiny.

Yet friends still came with bottles of wine.
        I looked splendid under the cherry tree once,

like a backward meteor. That smile, a flag
        that rips open the sky. Having not realized

at the time that collapsing is the only way to embrace,
        the whole tree turned white overnight.

Aria of an Ebbing Scene

Four o'clock in the afternoon, Ignacio Sánchez
             Mejías starts to trim his nails.
In the way Bernini carves the laurel buds
             from a marble's edge, or Canova
uses the material of death to shape lust. Flesh
          is a fleeting skiff, emptied to be
sustained on the stream, or is a Chinese porcelain
             aging in its perpetual patterns.
Look, how the almond turns bitter in the wind,
             the way evenings hollow out a man
who lowers his chin to drink from expired feeling.
             His pale hands interlock
like two boys drowning in inchoate language.
             The mechanism of the pendulum
is a perennial instant, but the clock is not the time.
             At midnight, the snow-blade
of waves whittles out a bronze horse.
             We can't stop the vanished
beings from turning into a string of muted wind-bells.
             Waking, we say the cemetery
is a large summerhouse or a leaving train, loaded
             with too many unredeemed doings.
But friend, think twice—is it not cruel
             to talk about wintry ice
             to midsummer mayflies?

贰 II

江	River
溪	Stream
共	Share
石	Stone
根	Root

Beethoven

Deep autumn, my neighbor starts to wonder
how am I going to live. I want to die.
Life has depleted its sustenance. No telephone.
No texts from you. I listen to Beethoven,
learning how to go on even if I'm betrayed
by the present. In two hours
it's going to rain. The streets will be completely bare.
The world grotesque like a stretcher.
Future full of meanness, vatic with voids.
Late sonatas of Beethoven are different
from his earlier works, his more familiar,
famous lessons on strength and light.
Pedagogical arpeggios. Polished by time
and torments of time, like a leaf stuck
in the windowpane, Sonata no. 31, for example,
is but a magpie with its wings and tail chopped off.
Even if you don't want life, you live by eating,
sleeping, loving without an object.
You pray and your prayer comes true. All this
is but a dream of feathers. I wait for the pianist's
fingers to slide back into her pockets.

Preludes, a Blue Plume

1

The young boys' beauty pains me, sharp-tasting like new lemons
is a line from Adélia Prado that I would like to use for my epitaph.

2

It was the soft hand of a young man
that dragged me back to this sensual world.

3

In three days, he will die
in a car crash. You never know.

4

Instead, people lug their dumb heads in streets, streets
that float upon the brass color of erosion, mixed
with flaxen lamps and the dark green of linden trees.

5

Each blossom is an overlord
of suicide. No one can help.

6

Whenever I am in grief I memorize Lorca and hum along to Bach.

7

When you return you will not
know your face in the mirror.

8

Tonight, great engineers calculate grief—its amazing modulus
of elasticity—with which they will build a blank tower,
then a highway to a more solid soul against this material world.

9

Erosion is a blossom, reversed.

10

The ruling ideas are nothing more than the ideal expression
of the dominant material relationships, the dominant material relationships
grasped as ideas, said Marx.

11

This form we trust so deeply to be good.
And days and nights ruled by your eyelids.

12

Remember that long-legged boy beside the doorstep, in white
shirt flaring against the peeled pine, smoking, his sweated
neck the color of glazed copper; soon that, too, will be dust.

13

The relatives, friends still weeping
The strangers, already singing
Where shall I leave this body
Parts of a mountain, parts of snow

Is a poem I translated, by Tao Yuanming,
so beautiful I'd like to use it here for you.

14

As if tears with their little arms
could lift you out of death.

15

When you return / I will trade my face / For your mirror.

16

Not a coffin
to hold your past. I have it all
in my head, making my flesh and bones
your shifting tombstone.

Incoherent Funeral March

Imagine you are a violinist, a true maestro,
beside a peopleless piano, perpetually
fiddling Bach's solo. Now imagine you are
the violin—without the hand, a broken thing.
Imagine you are the hollowness inside
the instrument as the fiddler wrestles
to assemble notes. Imagine in this fermata,
your eyes a thigh-deep pond, where a star-
stabbed stallion—whose hank of thick
tail is yet to be mended into the bow hair—
neighing, neighs for a departure he didn't bid.

Fish

It wasn't I who killed the fish.
　　　　It was the soup. It was a sin to drink it.
Not to mention the flesh. A greater sin.
　　　　A greater indulgence.
By the kitchen sink, my aunt held a fish
　　　　as if holding the Holy Body.
A shaft of sun leaned in to behold
　　　　the scene, to assist the sacrifice
by turning into a knife, shelling the fish
　　　　flake after flake. The fish thrashed
like a lamb. I thought it was a lamb.
　　　　Small one. A sincere sacrifice.
My aunt nodded, granting this convulsion
　　　　a gentle consent. After all,
it was a clean doing. No blood. Only
　　　　the white scales descended
like pear blossoms, wafting the metallic scent
　　　　of snow. That's how lingchi
was invented 1,000 years ago by some
　　　　wise Chinese. A sinner was put
to death by slicing 3,600 pieces of flesh
　　　　from the body. This slow slicing
was recorded as an indulgence to watch.
　　　　I watched this fish—blue were its eyes,
wide open like two wintry mountains.
　　　　"It is an art to cook the soup,"
says my aunt. This sweet stew of milk
　　　　thickens as I churn. The soup white.
So white, as if all our sins will be washed
　　　　when we drink it. The body
of the fish intact. It seems we've only borrowed
　　　　the fish to produce this white soup.
And it will come back to life as soon
　　　　as I put it into water. It *is* in water.

"Drink it hot," my aunt says, "the flesh
          is soft." This flesh tender,
some old hunger dies in my mouth.
          I remember years ago my Buddhist
mother took me to Tsethar, a religious
          ceremony to release the captive fish.
And there was one small fish, who
          barely knew how to swim, lingering
between my fingers as I stroked its scales.
          It wiggled a few inches away,
then back into my palms. I stroked it
          again. And again. Until it learned
everything about the water, everything
          about leaving. Leaving, I heard
the water thrashing behind me. The fish
          leapt out of the lamb-white water,
like a gull, to give me a last glance.
          The water riffled like those white
April flowers, or snow itself, falling
          and rising again. I think of this fish
while chewing the meat. It grew up.
          Grew larger. Like a child.
I think of it: the way its skin burned
          my hands like charred jade. Its eyes
inhaled all the blueness of the pond.
          Of sweetness my tongue drowns.

Being and Time

To see the lotus pond behind a pinewood shrine,
the old man climbs to the top of mountains.
He points to that void in front of him.
"Are those lotuses or people? Or these are
the people, those lotuses?" Pointing to this void
beside him. It has passed the lotus season,
which he spent with his dying wife. Half blind,
the wind strings the creeks into one clink
of a jade ring. A mallet making the bronze
bell tremble. The monks chant. The youngest
one, dozing most of his morning, lifts his
eyelids: that pond full of startled egrets, flitting.

Chaconne

Whether 无 emptiness is equivalent to 空 nothingness is a question
this child will consider in twelve years when he becomes a youth monk
in the temple nearest his hometown. But this afternoon, let him be
a child, let him drown the ants with his spit, knead their gasters till
his fingers are stained with their dark liquid, which he licks clean & whose
bitterness will stick on his tongue as long as his tongue is red as his kāṣāya.

Tonight, as this youth monk repents his sins—of killing two soldiers
who stabbed his mother in her womb, his unborn sister—he thinks that
the two bullets he planted in the soldiers' scalps with the touch of his
forefinger are as exquisite as the ants. He cannot understand that adding
twelve grams of metal to the bodies of two young men his age could stop
them from breathing; just as he could not understand the ants' death.

The temple, built in the Song dynasty, is made of pine wood, splendid
on the outside, while on the inside there is as much vacantness as
completion. The perennial scent of incense, the oil lamps' green fire,
burning like jade beads, fill just enough of the absent presence, enough
to accommodate both the ants and soldiers behind the draped eyelids
of the young monk, who is still, in fact, a child, who toys with his prayer
beads and chants the sūtras as some sad love songs. He knows by heart,

even though he refuses to know, the teaching of the Diamond Sūtra; he
knows that 无 emptiness, contingent upon the fabric of impermanence,
exists while 空 nothingness, as it is, doesn't. His heart is a hole. As he
repents, tears stream from his pupils, black as the ants, leaden as the bullets
that had perforated (quiet resemblance to 空 nothingness) the soft flesh
of two boys who had hollowed his mother's womb. 空 nothingness—
if it did not happen, if the cavities could be filled—does not exist.

He tries to go back to the afternoon to save the ants from his own fingers.
He tries so hard that he becomes one of the ants, and from the ant's eyes

he sees that beside this killing, there is a cluster of lilies, tear-streaked, shivering in the wind, which look almost like the face of his unborn sister, of whom he dreams nightly. And the emptiness of lilies' slim bodies somehow replaces the space that once resided in nothingness.

Easier to Lift a Stone Than to Say Your Name

What will you do
when you see

a woman's palms
forming

a cemetery
carrying a canary

Will you weep
Will you sweep

the rain-slain
peach blossoms

back to the root
of their tree

Calligraphy

I remember each furrow of your hand : even as I recite each line of your book
On the flyleaf, my grandfather's signature is well rendered with a fountain
pen. A gesture of holding. I mull over his calligraphy from fifty years ago:
his name, three characters of cursive script pouring, splashing like the sparse
trace of bamboo. The ink is blue black, the leaves yellowing. The kinds of
colors that take half a century to precipitate and fade. He once told me, *In
the distance, the southern hills discuss whether to give a rain.* Now I mimic his
calligraphy with rains of dots and strokes: the dash that drips like a peony
dew, the slant skimming like a sword. I'm no good at those techniques after all:
Strange Stone, Jade Table, Iron Pillar, Pincer of a Crab, Tiger's Tooth, Horn
of Rhinoceros, Bird Pecking, and Golden Knife. I hold my breath, wrestle
line by line. Within the structure of characters, strokes take breath from
one another, rendezvous like lifelines on our palm prints. Now that I have
taken time to practice I realize how differently we write the same character
in our names, our surname, with different stroke order, different pauses, and
different degrees of curves. It seems we are mismatched by our surname, the
gesture of holding generations of belongings in four cursive strokes. When I
flip the leaves, the book sends forth—autumn, I think. It's the autumn during
the Cultural Revolution when my grandfather met his girl.

Strange Stone : dashed too thick
You were sent to the far north. You were among intellectuals targeted by the
Red Guards. In the rural labor camp, she gave you two babies: a boy and a girl.

Jade Table : stroked too stale
You stamped out a forest fire, your hands burned, trembled for the rest of
your life. You couldn't pick up calligraphy. Since then, your brush pens were
stranded like August branches, drooping with osmanthus blossoms. That
spring, I watched your desolate inkstone slowly infuse with pear-blossom
rain. You stood by the window. Said nothing.

Horn of Rhinoceros : skimmed too thin
For the rest of your life, you hid a box of candy under your pillow. She had low
blood glucose. You planted a garden of peonies for her. You said, *The peonies*

are all about waiting, and that is the reason they bloom like lanterns, beacons for
the return.

Golden Knife : too sharp

You loved poetry, a terrible hobby. You embezzled the money for candy, bought a secondhand Du Fu collection, bargaining all afternoon. You got hustled. How I remember, you laughed and clapped when I recited Lu You's poem. I'd never seen you so proud, reticent man. Having not read the poems that I wrote, too soon you boarded the forgetful boat.

The name no longer uttered : always remembered

I flatten the folded page of the book, then refold it, to trace your warmth. It's gone. Those last days in the white hospital room, your palm swelled, tender as a ripened fruit or the torn pages of a fallen book. Your palm swayed and swayed like a landing crane beside the snowy bedsheets. With a last tremor of warmth you stroked my cheek—finishing your final calligraphy. Listen, reticent man: here, I recite my poem for you.

Requiem

March evening
blades of rain

unveil
apricot blossoms

dropping them
like little skulls

All night
the moon

sutures
wounds between

linden trees
It takes

seven seconds
for a petal to drop

Seven years
for us to mourn

轰隆隆 Is the Sound of Thunder

滴滴答答 is the rain stitching a bell jar, or the clock remembering its days
as a clepsydra. 扑通 is the sound of a man stumbling
& 哈哈哈哈 is the laughter that chases after
玲玲琅琅 is the water sword whacking the 哐当锵锵 jade pendants
of cold rocks. 飒飒瑟瑟 is the west wind & 扑扑簌簌
is the falling leaves that 萧萧翩翩 with an autumnmoon

In fact, 簌簌 is the sound of all soft things falling
The tears 簌簌 on the face. The snow 簌簌. The begonia 簌簌
on the mahogany bone of a folding fan. 簌簌 the brushstroke
paints the rice paper into a landscape of black mountains
冷冷淙淙 the rivers flow where the inked mountain is not depicted
flow in the uncharted whiteness

The bold strings 嘈嘈 like blizzard, the fine strings 切切 like murmur—
the melody of a girl playing 琵琶 on the orchid boat
back in the Tang dynasty which we still hear through 白居易's poetry

If the river could speak, would the mountain understand its utterance

The sound of a frog is 呱呱呱, which is annoying
If you cannot stand the 呱呱呱, please put the frog into a boiler
The hard part: try not to mourn the frog

The sound of the autumnmoon is 寻寻觅觅, 冷冷清清
凄凄惨惨戚戚, which is also the 点点滴滴 sorrow of 李清照

Because to mourn the frog one must speak in the language of frog
which is to 呱呱呱

咿咿呀呀 is a 青衣 singing with 盈盈脉脉 lips of red beans
飘飘冉冉 is their furbelow 依依霏霏 among the willows & catkins

式微 is the evanescent light of a lantern. Wrong. 式微 is the swansdown
evening, a girl calling her beloved: Why don't you come back? Come back

In truth, 式微 is 王维 writing a poem to the shadow of his leaving friend
who promised to come back with a sprig of magnolia to light up the yard
His poem has the sound of clouds spread low on the moving water

The lamplight threads a dim song across the voice of trees
that can only be heard by insects & birds

关关喈喈雍雍嘤嘤嗷嗷萋萋肃肃呖呖 are the sounds of birds
薨薨喓喓嘒嘒趯趯啁啾了了 are the sounds of insects
噼里啪啦 are the firecrackers bumping into the air
叽里咕噜 is a mouse stealing oil & falling from the chair
呦呦 the deer sings. 萧萧 the horse chases the wind
淅淅沥沥 the knuckles of rain knocking windows of a departed train
知了 is the cicada chirping its name: 知了知了
布谷 is the cuckoo calling itself: 布谷 cuckoo cuckoo 布谷

For us, the petals fall with no sound. For the fire ants, the petals hit
the ground with a sound as loud as thunder, which is 轰隆隆

But what is the ant's onomatopoeia for the thunder & falling flowers
What is the petal's onomatopoeia for the wind that brings forth its own falling
Still, we keep hearing, hearing, hearing the hiss of white, yellow
& blue petals scattered in a bowl bitten by the ants' bitter teeth

淅沥沥 淅沥沥 淅沥沥 淅沥沥 the rain
轰隆隆 轰隆隆 轰隆隆 轰隆隆 the thunder

Utterance of a Folding Fan

the missing bones are carved
by wind : the wind is a rickety
chime, chattering : moths captured
in a lamp : the sleeplessness

congeals a mirror : the mirror
calls : a silvery voice is broken :
water drips from the crack :
bones are filled with dark wax

& cannot make a sound : the orchid
is a grievous girl, tapping a nightly
mountain temple : a fan is opened
by time : the orchid drawn out

of the sheath forges into a sword
cutting streamlines of water :
the fan is closed : plums fall, crickets
weave shattered scales : mayflies

live for descendants : the white
gown on the boat plays a flute :
a river filling with maple leaves
listens to the evening bell

Through the Darkness

of night find me through the darkness
I am here I promise

find me through the night I am here
I promise the same

darkness the stark attendance of stars
above the water I am

here in the darkness find me I promise

Time the Stone Makes an Effort to Flower

Why are we asked to cut
into this realm of red dust?
In the Southern dynasty,
the stars shine bronze swords
upon an eddying evening,
knifing the orchid patterns
over the waist of mountains,
where monks, under oil lamps,
recite the Heart Sūtra.
Their tenuous effort
to harden hearts into rocks.
Their bodies round
by the nightpours becoming
raw plums with no branch
to untwist from.
To reflect is to hold
all the remembered longings
that are lost by time,
and to deflect is to meet
all forgotten faces,
which are eventually one face.
A thousand overlapping
eyelids of hydrangea
are a thousand winecups
beside your grave.
I have no intention to make this
an elegy. Part of me is dead
with you, let that be
the elegy. Part of me so alive—
so extra. All night, ached
by my arms—the unplucked
strings of a lyre : liars
to their own body—I am lured
into clasping an opening

that was once the shape
of you. Parchments of desire,
illegible scribbles—salt line
on your blighted thigh.
Teach me the dark art of doldrums.
Teach me to survive with one
posture like a pebble
in streaklines of river.
But if something survives
the fire, survives
the destruction of forms,
will you walk to me
in this destroyed blue,
as I walk to you
for the rest of my time,
barefoot. Will you touch me,
your finger bones then
synthesized with stems
of chrysanthemums. Will you
return to me
my desire, burning
for the two worlds to meet?

叁 **III**

早 　　Dawn

霞 　　Glow

随 　　Trace

類 　　Existence

影 　　Shadow

Vermeer: Thief

Staying at a person's house. Without the person present. Is what
a thief does. A profession: to take without permission. To be

with no possession. A persimmon. Turning sweet. Like a peach.
All fruits the same desire. A gesture of lure. That the gone master

uses. To bait guests. Expression without volition. To be touched.
The thief enters. Sets aside his gloves. To peel persimmons.

The way he peels a slant of evening light. It is all too late. The fruit
is not a certain bait. The thief's hand. A gesture of castaway.

Taking away a thing. That is not there. Doesn't make it stealing.
This firm fruit on the canvas of dark blue. Of mind's deep sorrow.

A song that asks the longing for a fruit. To replace the fruit.
Imagine this thief, now a boy with smudged face, stepping

inside that blueness. Hanging his small body like a clean shirt
to the same railing. A skeleton dream to take apart. To put together

a skyline in blue. Distant. Defined against sky. Where roofs waltz
like an ever-departing sea. Ever returning. So blue it could be

swallowed like a pill. In such blueness. Who dreams of me.
Will his dream damage me. What's left for imagination is what

stays forgotten. A thief took away the persimmon. What remains.
The boy once peeled. The alloy of some unspeakable softness.

A Difficult Apple

1/ Odd is the poor apple who doesn't know it's the center of the world.
   If it was soft enough, it'd be a tomato. An apple
   it is—legal and proud—a fine citizen of the apple kingdom.

2/ Last night at a bar on Sixth Street, you, my friend, melancholy.
   "What's wrong?"   "Nothing."

3/ It is difficult to know what the apple is thinking.

4/ The glassy meadow covered
   with crests of egrets. A lake
   lacerated by the thin disk of sun.

5/ Instead, we talked about Mozart and his unfinished Requiem.
   The commendatore scene in *Don Giovanni* is a masterpiece; so
   were your bored, patient hands tucking the napkin into a swan.

6/ "What's wrong?"

7/ The roadside cherries and the gazing plums
   are trading their darkening lips and tongues.

8/ *Even a piece of white napkin is political,* my critical theory friend once told me.

9/ I start to worry about my apple. It doesn't respond.
   Its cold skin repulsive. Its body, beatless.
   I put the apple in my pocket and run to the hospital.

10/ *The apple possesses nothing,* said my father, *it stands with the proletariat.*

11/ Taxi at night is expensive—washed nickels of stars
    —with an apple in my pocket, I possess two hearts.

12/ At the age of five, Mozart wrote Minuet and Trio in G Major.
    In 1791, he wrote his final masterpiece, Requiem in D Minor. From G to D—
    it's clear—he didn't get that far in his career.

13/ The ubiquitous light catches the fallen
insects; they are the hieroglyphs
on pamphlets of an insomniac cypress.

14/ My lips pressed against my friend's locked lips. I thought,
in this way, I'd know what he was thinking. I made three
discoveries: 1st, my friend is a professional kisser.
2nd, my friend prefers peppermint gum. 3rd, "nothing."

15/ My critical theory friend told me, *You're shallow as a shadow,*
you have no depth. I agree. But cast by whom?

16/ Advice for an adjusted desire—
                    according to mythology—if
                                 you see an *apple* in *Paris*—be
careful—you can't be sure which
                    one wants to have sex with you.
                            Let no war be waged because of you.

17/ Shallow as a shadow? That's a terrible simile.

18/ I am angry. The apple is difficult to communicate with. It is a
difficult apple, perhaps even political. This is a political apple.

19/ Even Rostropovich's dead cello won't tune a sad note for this bad apple.

20/ In fact, with its skin red as a flag, I suspect
                it is a communist apple. No wonder
it doesn't talk. Its whole body, *The Gulag*
             Archipelago, incarcerates few kernels.

21/ When I made love to another man, I thought of my friend's forelocks
wet with sweat. But he's just a friend. He's no different from another apple.

22/ Inside the apple's jailed soul—four kernels. Four soldiers
    in battalions of snow. Four artists in Siberia's correction camps
    chewing straws. Four Syrian children on an exiled boat
    in Mediterranean passage. Four little Odysseuses. Four
    masterless dogs. Four dogless masters finding their dogs.

23/ Hard to imagine that in their previous lives the apples
    are some pale pink blossoms that open like infants' palms.

24/ Phosphorescent meadow. Jade sea.
    Lambs carrying frost. Amorous cherries
    petting slim shoulders of a fox. 4 a.m.

25/ Convinced by my friend that the apple is a government, I slit its throat
    open. I give the camped kernels names: Solzhenitsyn, Shostakovich,
                                        Mandelstam, Rostropovich.

26/ By consciousness, we are separated
    from the world. Separated from
    each other. Without volition, without
    us, the apple conquers the world.

27/ "I prefer red apples to green apples," I say.
    My critical theory friend, "Are you a racist?"

28/ *What's even worse than a flute? Two flutes!* (Mozart)
    Now I have two apples. My life is miserable.

29/ In my last life, I must have been some pale pink flowers.

30/   "Not really. Just a communist."

31/ Someday we will be given the same apple
        we had once eaten. Of the same dream,
    chaw after chaw, we realize we are dreamers.

32/ 6 a.m. at Heathrow Airport, my aunt texted me: *if I die, please take care of your little cousin, my son.*

33/ DON GIOVANNI
　　Leporello, ove sei?

　　LEPORELLO
　　Son qui, per mia disgrazia, e voi?

　　DON GIOVANNI
　　Son qui.

　　LEPORELLO
　　Chi è morto, voi o il vecchio?

DON GIOVANNI
Leporello, where are you?

LEPORELLO
I'm here, unfortunately, and you?

DON GIOVANNI
Over here.

LEPORELLO
Who's dead, you or the old man?

34/ What my aunt really said was, 如果我不在了, meaning *if I am not here,* or *if I am here no longer,* both of which are false propositions— she has never been anywhere near anyone—but the phrase can also be translated as *if I cease to be,* which I understand and question at the same time: why is my family full of crazy women? Sometimes I wonder if I, too, am a crazy woman, who has attempted multiple suicides, like other women in my family, all for the cause of screwed-up men, but I suspect she is not going to do it this time, for she just had a baby, and I understand her worry of age, but when she said her baby was diagnosed with autism, I became her apple and had no idea what she was talking about.

35/ In French the apple is *pomme.* Is this a poem? No, this is an apple.

36/ My friend gave me the origami. Despite its neck like the stem of a lily, its pleated-petal wings, the swan is unmistakably a napkin.

37/ Listening to Shostakovich on Apple Music, I realize why apples never try to become men.

38/ I soon find out that my cousin may not have the skill of language
   or communication, meaning he may call the washer his father,
   meaning when I call his name he may not respond, meaning
   he's in his own world, meaning I cannot translate my world
   to him, meaning he will be lonely without feeling lonely,
   meaning these meanings may have no meanings to him at all,
   meaning my little cousin may just be another difficult apple.

39/ With its amputated freedom
   the apple is now a knuckle
   of a chain, arresting my eyes.

40/ Powerless to practice flight, the napkin-swan
   transforms the glass table into a pond.

41/ In 1970, Rostropovich sheltered Solzhenitsyn and was later exiled
   from the Soviet Union for his inappropriate generosity. Instead
   of being political, the tone of his cello is rather unbearable. They
   sat on the dim chairs, ate rotten apples together in an unlit room.

42/ In 2018, which was last summer, I held my cousin in my arms
   and rocked gently. I kissed his shaved head. He was so small,
   so light, so *not-here*. His chest a little drum. When he woke,
   looked at me, his eyes pond-deep, I didn't realize what our eyes
   had carried for us were just two different, difficult realities.

43/ Autumn evening
   the world almost completes
   itself with dragonflies'
   imminent execution
   in light rain—
   they stagger a little longer

44/ Another melancholy night in November,
   my friend and I sat in the bar. "What's wrong?"

45/ When we are talking about Mozart we are really talking about *Don Giovanni,* which is perhaps the darkest piece our chubby Wolfgang ever composed, except for the introduction of his Piano Concerto no. 20 in D Minor k 466, that is to say we are in fact talking about the death of his father, poor Mr. Leopold Mozart, so to put it another way— instead of talking about an apple, we are talking about the apple tree— therefore, Don Giovanni is Mozart himself and is a hero in purgatory because he won't repent for murdering Donna Anna's father, yelling at the statue of the ghost, *No, no, ch'io non mi pento. Vanne lontan da me!* —what an asshole—so to summarize, instead of talking about an apple tree, we are really talking about the fall of an apple.

46/ The apple does not think, hence
the apple does not exist. I think
I exist as a part of the apple's unthinking.

47/ Someday the words you speak will become things.
You'll say, *apple.* And you'll choke
with a red globe in your throat. I'll gouge it out.
Put it in my mouth. But if you say something else,
something I can't handle—for example, *love*—
does it mean you'll vomit yourself inside out?

48/ I took the apple out of my pocket,
a slow explosion, a real fruit,
hot, not an abstraction of thought.

49/ *Stay with me to-night; you must see me die. I have long*
had the taste of death on my tongue, I smell death, and who
will stand by my Constanʒe, if you do not stay?
(Mozart)

50/ Trying to figure out what I'm thinking, my friend kisses me.
Fingers latching into my hair. We are suddenly two fleshly apples,
conversing through the dark, ignorant language of fruits.

51/ Whose hand is it that wakes me from the tree?
Whose lips inlaid in my skin? For whom am I severing
my sweet limb into whose strange body?

52/ The apple before me / never attempts to convince me / it is an apple.

A Bulldozer's American Dream

At the construction site the bulldozer works
days & nights. No, it is the man inside who works.
The man & his machine are one. After the stars
& dogs & coffees brewed with hands of his loved one,
her night hair of soft river, of his own volition
the man chose to participate in this heavy-lifting labor.
Wrong, it's the machine that does. No more
than twenty-five: the man, forearm knotted, grips
the handle & the machine's hydraulic stick follows—
an extension of his body & to that extent, his mind.
His mind, as we know it, does not want to be a man,
or anything with a preconceived structure.
But how can he resist this pleasure, his thighs
harvesting, his glazed nape taut as a stag's skin,
discharging summer rain. It is the mind that cannot
resist this sweet perk of the earth. It is the mind
that tames the bulldozer's tender monstrosity & orders
it to pick up, with connivance, those dusk-damaged
bones for its master & dig into the deep-delved
darkness, an interior otherwise unattainable.
Some evenings, the man leaves the construction site
for steaks & candles & wine thick as plagued blood,
musing the neck of his wife, whose good flesh
is continuous as his dreams in which the earth
will never betray him, for he is its filial son,
competent at his duty: *Fill the earth & subdue it.*
Then the machine, without its master, lowers its bucket
in rain. Then through the hard latticework of this city,
its metal drilled by a known silence. It hurts to look at it.
A sad thing. The machine still is not a part of anything.

Reliquary Evening

He picks up his pen and digs
                             into this untranslatable
world again—with the inscrutable crutches of syntax
and prepositions, he thinks
                             he has extracted a tincture
of sweetness from the earth—pure objects, each
purely its own subject.
                             Speechless. Solemn terror.
For example: shadow, the pasted isolation of a dog, or
a streetlamp, emptied with light,
                             is the conqueror
of an encapsulated sunrise, etc. Though soon he finds
that he merely misinterprets
                             this landscape
like a dull literary critic. This grandiose text of an arched,
apparent incomprehensibility.
                             Soon he finds
that conjunctions, reaping no correspondent forms in this clean-
limbed world, are closest
                             to divinity. He knows
it is not the world that is untranslatable but himself—
his hands mutilate
                             into fingers, into touch—
himself being his own object for observation, his feelings
are less than a joke.
                             If he is to be flattened
on the page, he doesn't want to be a word, not even *moon*
or *rose,* their quiet, scentless
                             resemblance to vanity.
He wants to be an equation, logical, cold, its vigilant gaze
knowing precisely its own destiny.

Meditation on an Authentic China

I'll be rude. Since there's no proper name to call such an ill-
mannered thing—its varnished skin resembles no thing
but a porcelain vase—I call it china. I call it china, though really
it was manufactured in West India, or Venezuela, or any
third world country by a child's hands mudded in a makeshift
workshop beside a brushwood door, where the child's dog
(not his pet, his dog) chases a lime butterfly. Let us call
the child the artist & his dog the guardian of art. Nevertheless,
the child must report a failure in his artistry. Painted
with lanky figures dressed in suits & two limousines shuffling
beneath streetlights of fruits. He calls it china. Perhaps
it portrays the child's dream of the first world. But where is
the orchid, the lantern, the rice-paper fan unveiling the face
of a vermilion girl whose hair must be pitch-black, whose eyes
must be filled with tragedy? Is it true that through tragedy
we are cleansed & transfigured, the way a stone is honed
into a jewel? The stone remains a stone. Crystal & uncut,
the child still a child in his village. While we, transformed
by our love for commercials & shop windows through which
we dream of the dreams dreaming us, are as foreign
& real as a man drinking whiskey on a camel in the Kalahari.
Lavender-scented shampoo suggests a well-meaning civilization.
Each night I civilize my pitch-black hair. Buy me. I am
a product of your estranged wanting. Exchange me. I am
a wanting myself, estranged by your wanting, which is a product
of the promulgating posters in the street where the winter
is real as communism. Though the china is, in truth, real
& authentic, it seems less real for being not at all what you
imagined. Your china is more beautiful, more or less, like the jar
atop a mountain in Tennessee. *Like nothing else in Tennessee.*
After all, you are the artist. The child, a product of your artistry,
fails to fulfill your vision. The child is the china he made, filled
with false dreams. None of us will meet the child, will rinse
his mudded hands. None will know his name. His name is Hu.

Because who cares about Hu. Not even his parents who left
that southwest village to secure migrant jobs at a Shanghai
construction site, where the company provides no insurance
but (thank god) offers daily settlement. They'd buy the two-yuan
steaming-hot baozi & soy milk from a tricyclist at 5 a.m.,
just before the pouring of concrete, & pay a little extra
because the tricyclist's daughter was diagnosed with leukemia
a month ago & that reminds them of their son & daughter,
whom they have promised a brighter future, & that's why
they took the three-day train to Shanghai, work through the night
for the future of their children, disowning their present.
So for Hu, his government is his grandfather's walking stick,
his religion: his sister's braided hair swinging like a pre-autumn
bulrush. Each day, he'd walk behind her red-banded pendulum
for an hour & a half, past the creek of dead reeds, past
the bamboo alley, to his school, which he'd usually skip
& sneak to a kiln run by a local merchant, who, too,
has promised him daily settlement, so he can buy a blue
hairband for his sister, for blue is his favorite color, which is
the shade of his mother's overwashed apron & of his
grandfather's silhouette when he chugs cups of home-brewed
sorghum wine like a ragged Li Bai in the yard where they
have planted medicinal herbs & camellias; how everything
loses its hues in the moonlight into deliquescent blue—
such beauty, such stillness echoing eternity, is only a quarter
inch from death, which will come in less than two years
when his father falls from the seventeenth floor, his cheekbone
pierced by two rebars, legs strapped on the freshly finished
concrete slab, creating an abstract arabesque pattern of blood
so ravishing his son is powerless to paint on his porcelain.
Without testaments, history is no more than a buried legend.
Years later when the boy's name is mistaken for Who,
instead of asking who is Hu, we might ask ourselves who
is Who? & instead of claiming Hu is real! we ask, who is real?
What is real here is the solitude of the china, of not being
understood by you. Its gaping rim doesn't utter a word

of frustration. Maybe this is a sign of suppression, of suffering
long under the regime of dictatorship. A valid premise.
For on the china's neck there's a dash of red, which must be
evidence of communism, which is likely another hypocritical—
excuse my English, *hypothetical* scenario assembled by dream
& out of the infected collectiveness of any dream's naïveté,
the argument proceeds: do the child's bruised hands constitute
him a certificate as an ideal citizen, purchasing dreams
from the nation's vending machine, or is to be ideal to have a self
smashed, a mind stout as the hooked meat in a butcher shop,
readily minced for consumption, while still being convinced
that with a stem of daffodil one could burn down the castle?
Since when do these dreams, chosen out of desire, subjugate
the reality, or is it true that the reality is so somatic to our senses
that we require a collective fantasy to mitigate it? Convinced
by what we believe, we see with astral eyes, which situate us
in an idealized world through which each of us becomes the object
of our own imagination, glamorous & possibly free, authentic
for sure, because some of us are, by others, then desired,
even momentarily, in this glorious catnap of democracy.
If to be authentic is somehow to be partly true, which
in certain circumstances means to be naked & undisguised,
then the nakedness is not of the body but in our eyes. Tragedy
enters when dream breaches reality, which, luckily, occurs
to none of us, nor to the child, whose miseries seem no grander
than a situation comedy. Because rather than dreaming, we are
granted dreams. Even the dead refuse to wake up from them.
Someday our grandfathers, dressed in chanterelles & moss,
will fall into awakening & ask if communism has ultimately
been realized, if the red flags have taken root like the crepe
myrtle in a childhood backyard, not the dynasties with rice wine
of immanent ecstasy, or the inkwell stilled to instill a possible
masterpiece of calligraphy. The bamboo flute is buried
beside the pear blossoms that shred like broken snow.
It snowed briefly yesterday. Today, when Hugh is dragged
to the flea market in the East Village of Lower Manhattan

by his mother, who wants to celebrate his success, for yesterday
he got an acceptance letter from Princeton where he will
spend the next four years perfecting his craft in art & sculpture
& stuff, he comes across this china made by Hu & fondles
its cheap enamel with his slim, translucent fingers, well-preserved
by Patagonia mittens & L'Occitane hand cream. The porcelain
burns his palms with the same temperature as the winter sun.
His mother would like him to have this modest token.
But he's in a hurry. He decides to indulge his jubilance
among friends. His friends are calling. They are on their way
for linguine with shrimp scampi & some illicit beer, for one kid
is the nephew of the restaurant owner. He knows his way
to the cellar & his way to satiate. While Hugh is holding
hands with his girlfriend under the table, he cannot erase
from his mind the china whose coarse coldness leaves
his hands unscarred. He didn't accept the gift. He doesn't
need it. Hugh does not need to be validated by any object. No,
he doesn't need to prove himself real according to our imagination
as a lover would do, & by doing so, be made more beautiful.
Hugh *is* beautiful. His tipsiness paints a delightful blush.
He will not return home for dinner, though his mother
has cooked him his favorite ribs, & mushrooms stippled
with asparagus, which he would never touch, until he would—
after he fills her coffin with petals of his choice, primrose,
iris, camellia & snowdrop, in early November of the same year.
He will continue to hunger, continue to want & wonder
about Hu's china, whose ghastly craftsmanship & unrefined
sensibility will continue to startle him like the screech
of a blackbird shot through the midnight blue. Though Hugh
will never know why, he will return to the flea market
each Sunday, & he will never find the china, not even
a fragment, & he will look at his palm & imagine
his touch has become its last remains. & Hu will return
to his rancid creek & hopeless village, to his desk lamp
& cold noodles & the tombs of his father & sister, who died
of giving birth to a daughter, whose first name is *I,*

which means love. Hugh & Hu will continue to return to find
grief, find loss an inspiration that unknots this fabrication
of self & we will follow them. We will try to return to where
we are from, & fail, & it's not because the landscape
has been reassembled by factories or the early dreamscape
has vanished into misty air. Proceeding to our tragic return &
having returned, we return only to find we were never there.

Red

By the firewood door
I watch a monk who under plum
boughs sweeps shreds of red

the way this wintry shrine
sweeps all the forgotten travelers
into a crush of petals

brushing the shoulders
of statues, their senseless bodies
drowned in redness.

Beside the stone-arch bridge,
where every blossom is a storm.
In this world of red dust,

how do you know you are
seeing the darkness rather than being
blindfolded? Do you hear

the doe cry at nighttime?
To her, all falling materials replace
their flesh with water.

What Sustains in This Autumn Rain

It'd be nice to see a stray dog limping along
the sidewalk. So you understand that sadness
is not original. The dog curls cold in my mind
as an unlit wick, which you refuse to kindle.
Here, touch its waterlogged hair. The dog
won't bite, the dog is not looking for a bone.
But there is no dog, you say, it is just a puddle
in the middle of the road which I have mistaken
for a dog. Sometimes, pain does not acquire
a form. Sometimes, it is all right to cry
through another pair of eyes. The dog is there,
barking blue, its whole body a torn fabric
wringing in rain. Now you can see what I see—
the stray dog is happy, happy without any bones,
unchained, chasing after his imaginary master.

Comrade Mannequin

1

The cosmos from the telescope is not for me
to photo. But understand also, the sky
is not a timberland where I seek sorrow.
Once or twice in my life,
when my eyes were filled with the oceanic teal
of the shop window, nothing was more real
than you, Comrade Mannequin, striding
to greet me in your matchless contrapposto.
My Adonisian Ganymede, I am not your
horrendous eagle. I am not
your god. But the mead cup spilling
on your left palm. Can someone write a letter
to the supreme leader to clarify
that our camaraderie is nothing physical; it is
like that solicitude of Pessoa to his distant stars.

2

It is strange & lonely. Comrade Mannequin,
when I stand in front of you, against
the infinitude of glass, I feel that I am
a faint star persisting in an uninvited, hysterical
watching, while you make love
to particles of perfume around you—
Brownian motion—marinated piece
of plastic meat, permeated by whatever
is not you, not me. The world denies our coupling
like the mayor denies the egg yolk
of lamplight varnishing the tar of the river.
Comrade Mannequin, if you are so alone,
would you comb out this ocean with me?
I have plenty of fish & none
of them remembers how to survive in the sea.

3

I am not against you going to the war,
if you feel it's necessary to die. Don't worry
about your demonstrated skill
at dodging shrapnel. With light on your feet
your virtuosic still-dance is the cue
to stance & attitude. Put some clothes on.
You can't march to Shlozshina like this.
You haven't seen the snow yet, which hurts
more than bullets. When you return,
I will reassemble you. Will put makeup
on your mutilated face. Will not replace
a single part of you. If necessary,
saw off my legs & arms. But my eyes I keep.
How they lock you in this moment of leap.
Naked as a cricket, you know
nothing about how darkly
this world is going to make you sing.

4

Comrade Mannequin, are you afraid to be,
let's say, objectified. Or your greatest fear is to be
humanized. Have you voted
for the Popcorn President, who promised
a cauldron nation? Kroisos Kouros,
your perfected torso & your archaic
smile. More beautiful than any of my creepy
semblables. But not even you, with your paper-lantern
abdomen, your caved gaze, cascading
an indiscriminate illumination, can change
what's been done. You cannot
change. Your mechanical, crescent smile remains
even in destruction. The Greek boy ran & fell
& drowned by the seashore when catching fish.
People insist: he is a ship.

They are half right. His sandscraped, whitewashed
backbone an unfolded paper boat.

5

Adieu, farewell, bye-and-bye
to your go-then-go on legs or trains or planes
or cargo boats. I will stick around & scratch my toes
with my shirt tucked & sleeves rolled.
Await your arrival in a headful of moonlight,
or snow. If you come back headless,
you will be prized with a necklace. Come back
with one balletic leg. If you fail
to return, mail me your finger bone.
I have taken your position
at the Liberation Department of Democracy Mall.
I've drilled nails to the edges of my lips
to study your smile. Have welded my arthroses.
Through the numerous binoculars in focus,
you shall inhabit the history & I will be loved.

肆 **IV**

寒	Cold
水	Water
各	Each
依	Lean
痕	Wound

Serenade behind a Floating Stage

My friend called and said that sex saved him. He made me listen
to streets in the Philippines waking up in rain, panes and trees

repeating a low note of *C*—chorister, cage, a choir captures
the cadenza of falling cardamoms, then a quartz of quietude.

So eventually, it was the *Q*—queer, he said, the parched skin
of the quarryman, whom he loved briefly for an afternoon.

For so long, we've mistaken the *Q* for *C;* weeping, he then recited
a passage of the Śūraṅgama Sūtra, an odd, phonetic transcription

from the Tang dynasty. The power, he insisted, is in the sonance,
not in its meaning, its attachment. This persistent, desperate,

loud howl of August is but the insects' thirst for mating
and survival. The naked nearness of a swimming pool pulses

in blue, so artificial it seems real. Wrongness: for years, my life
depends on a false letter, and as consequence, instead

of the quiet, a cry drills the carnage of my heart. Had I chosen
the path of *Q*, its hidden "you" might have entered me

with a silence, to which my heart would yield as the hollow
inside an oboe. The cicadas continue practicing deft mastery

of invisibility. I join their quartet. Where the moon streaks through,
the night makes a sound of fabric being torn inside my head.

Dark and huge, it is frightening to be alive with a song in you.

In the Movie Theater

after Gustave Flaubert

They find a dark corner to sit. Behind them

the acoustic batt, glass wool of rouge. The movie is about

eros, about two men in love, then failing to love.

The kind that is banished in China, where they are,

in this impoverished town of a province in the west, famous

for its radish-beef noodles stippled with cilantro,

Han-dynasty battlefields on loess plateaus, grapes

& parched hands. The ceiling lights darken. So one moves

his clandestine hand to the other's denim shorts.

& he lets it happen. It's like having caterpillars throbbing

inside his leg veins, he thinks. His stomach cramps.

His hand arranges itself across the fly of the other's pants—

thin fabric of wool shaped muscular by his thighs.

Together they escape this town of dreadful tricycles,

blast-hole drills for coal, scandals & gossips stripped

like the featherless roosters at the market downstairs

from his mother's apartment. That is why the movie

is in a language they can't comprehend. French

or English or Italian sounds the same. Sharp consonants

like popcorn scraping their gums. One turns his face

to the walled darkness, as the handsome actors

walked to a church of Saint something, then a colored-pebble lane named after a philosopher or a poet,

then a bar of incredible botanical decor & the liquor—

why is it green?—then a cemetery of great men

who are said to have changed the world, but not theirs,

each tombstone a stately gaze beneath the cypresses,

its sign language of imminent loss, then the harbor

of tired ships, where kisses should have taken place

like fireworks, but did not—the hyacinths he bought

this morning are dying for tap water—so he invited him

for swimming next month when he comes back

from business in Ohio, America, though the other

couldn't practice his promise—he died for a reason

that borders on homoerotic cliché—& the movie

ended with a scene where the man returned to scatter

hyacinth petals on a body of water, like baby steps

of Saint Peter, he said, like steps of Saint Peter

walking to greet Jesus, who, this time, lets him drown.

The cinema smells of tobacco & piss. Scraps of napkin

tossed like the torn wings of butterflies, liquefied

in the touch of fluorescent lamps. One of them opens

his hand, asking for nothing, which he receives.

Two Cannot

It begins with the distance—the sea sharp to a point
of suffering—and proceeds, for the distance remains
insatiable—across the table a stem of violet flares—
against its desire, *this* is given to the distance, instead
of a river—a misheard prayer : whetting the crucian
carps tarnished with scruffs : their carnal closeness—
continuous as the demonstration of time, in other
words : longing, to that end : grief that doesn't constitute
the service of the violet, whose violaceous lacquer
is its only consequence—charged with a serrated
fringe, it annihilates the two parted figures : lovers,
with timorous bodies misnamed, calling each other
by the name of a single flower—report of a blasted
dream—fell and shattered on their way to raze—
leaving a trail of fragments : we discard dust—we river
the running : we violate—the violet, twisted in our
hearts, still crucial for the distance to be absolutely
meaningful : us galloping as we shatter and become

Thin Air

Watch: they hug, they kiss, they make love

as the distance wrings a black seam that swims

between them. Apart, then the air. Then

waiting for the air to end. The air ends.

The tenuous line resumes its labor of sewing

two separations. The bodies vanish, the seam

is left to etch the sightline. Now that I am in a place

safe from rapture and grief, I see the limit

we failed to recognize. The crack in things

as the sunset folds its face in the sea, the burning

that rips, the way spring rips open everything.

As the nearest beach by the motel particulated

in bloom, for a brief minute, I couldn't tell

the difference between you and the hemorrhaging

hibiscus. The thirst to escape as we galloped

toward the waves. We were children again,

minds full of sand dunes and oars that stayed

within hand's proposal of destruction.

Later you stood alone against the darkening

sky, adjusting thin muscles on your left arm

to trace the motion of gulls. I watched you

long, knowing you could not be changed

by the setting sun—your watertight contour

of opaque rigidity is the crack of light. Infiltrated

with its last crimson, your eyes are the first

crack of the sky, which couldn't be healed

even if you turned away. The sky cannot turn away.

When you turned to me, with salt line on your neck,

I was transfixed. Thirst is the crack of water.

You, the crack of my desire. The black

seam appears as our bodies pile and fold softly

into an eyelid. Later, the air between us opens

into an eye, arresting light-years across plunging

constellations. We were almost transformed,

yet we stayed. Saved by our limit, we return

to folding socks, packing for our respective

livings that promise loneliness. That the border

is the beauty we live for. Is closest to our ruin.

Lie Beyond

One would always fall in love with the man
beside Jesus in any seventeenth-century oil painting,
preferably Flemish so that the tone is darker,
cold, therefore one inch closer to eternity.
The man is either passing a jar of water,
doling loaves of bread, or weeping carelessly,
like a dog, beside Jesus's feet. His left ankle
dissolves into the darkish purple shadow
of a cypress, his face half-seen, and that
makes him more beautiful. Though, Jesus, too,
I confess, *must* be beautiful, but I cannot love
a man with bearded chin like my father,
and to fall in love with a protagonist
forebodes tragedy. I want life I can cope
with easily, like washing watercress at a sink.
The weather in mind is so lovely this afternoon,
one can saunter into any museum and fall
in love with figures that are not human.
Isn't it what we do after all. Without
imagining his red-and-brown vestment
falling down, the garment his very skin,
voluptuous, percolated with tears, I find him
more seductive, perilous. Maybe he is a saint,
or something like, who has no desire
for earthly bodies, the way I do most days,
studying your sandals at the doorstep, conceptualizing
you whole, or tonight, with your back
turned to me, spine white in the moonlight,
pretending to lie beyond my attention.

La Traviata

He and he, almost indistinguishable in features because of their youth,

have reached a resolution to return their bodies to the dampened evening

as the nightingale coughs the last blob of black blood from its gullet,

wailing words it couldn't comprehend, *a quell'amor ch'è palpito, del-*

l'universo intero, while throwing its whole body to become that *palpito,*

the throb that shakes the universe in pieces by first fracturing its wings

into a glint of the bluish twilight on your ankle. Because you selected

the disc to revive Maria Callas while I was undressing, examining

the pimple on my chin, and you, being considerate, turned off the lamp

so I wouldn't be embarrassed by the images in your eyes. Hurry

and hush before the evening slowly chafes them into irreparables;

like those damaged equestrian statues in an antiquities store which stride

with a secondhand passion, he came into that darkness He brought—

stabbed, shapeless flowers. Did Violetta, after all her coughs and blood

and her unwanted throbs of love, wasting her coloratura on a total

douchebag, realize that all this floss and flick of an entertaining tragedy

is uncalled for, is in exchange for a crowd of strange hands, laughter,

whistles usurping tears, or, at most, a shock of white camellias at her graveyard. Unlike Violetta, he is not prepared to be a martyr of His lust.

He'd rather be that carriage, or that horse in front of that carriage, or

that pebble under the hooves of that horse, or that grass that trembles

like a staccato, no he doesn't want to be that famous soprano.

His left palm already the fermata of His aria. Dark blue evening sky

fixated by nails of silver. You hummed along to the "E strano!

E strano!" aria, a true maestro, while I, with my heart sunk into you

like a stone, a professional prostitute, felt my skin untouched by

the bird's screech, the trees imitating our serpentine bodies—all I want

is a moment of not being myself, and you, who repairs my body

with your body, who are no more than a cool shade where I open

myself to a soft indifference of the world. I do not love you and you

do not me. Though when I turn my face back from the window, with

your face in my hands, it is through your eyes the universe sees itself.

Tether

The tea is turning cold.
        It holds a winter in its mind.
                Soon, it will be a mattress

of dead pool and the beetles
        will lather their brittle shells
                in this blue bathroom.

The birds continue sighing,
        "I'd rather, I'd rather."
                I write to make myself un-

recognized. Inside the sterilized
        window, the spruce
                stays, magpies, erased.

The mountains are approaching.
        My lines must be
                revised, because you

were right: "It's best to read Russian
        novels in winter: it is always
                snowing. Everyone is sad."

Nude Descending a Staircase

"When I take off my bra, I'm unfettered like a soaring warbler,"
my cousin told me while slipping off her straps in front of a mirror.
Her hair was unbound. Her naked spine arching. The air outside
smoldered with the chirping of insects.

        I felt bashful watching her
        hair-shaded nape.
Her cardamom-like nipples bloomed in the mahogany frame
of the mirror. She felt at ease. Perhaps she thought I was still
too young? That I was more of a boy than a man?
Or perhaps she saw that day, by the rosemary alley,
a boy kissing my lips. He tasted like blueberries.

        The sudden rain stopped my thinking.
        The sudden rain stopped the flirting
of summer birds, shaping a formless cage.
"This rain ruined my day, & my date.
I'm supposed to be at a party by now," she said, brushing her hair,
appreciating her reflected flesh, her lips two slices of a plum.
As if in the mirror she were admiring that painting by Duchamp.
As if she were trying hard to decode her body; the breeze
from the ventilation fluttered her hair

        as she looked outside—
        at the yellowish lampposts,
the road luxuriant with oil. And then
she sang as if to become a cello wholly would help
to recognize her untuned body. As if by giving up
her shape she expressed her shape fully. Her hourglass waist.
& the rain like sand falling.

        Could this afternoon & the afternoon
        of yesterday be understood
through her moving body? She sang as if the world
depended on her tongue, the way musicians depend on their
instruments. Though what holds her here in front of me is still a mystery.
Was it my eyes fixing her in an articulated design, the mirror
suspending her escape, her skin of cello-lacquered membrane,

or her glowing eyes reverencing her flesh, decoding
Nude Descending a Staircase?

                          Or perhaps it was the air,
                          only the air that mattered.
As Duchamp put it himself, "The whole idea of movement,
of speed, was in the air." She would have wept
if she'd seen the painting, a headless cello
moving through a forest of many solid, tangible
geometries of loneliness & desire—
a dream constituted entirely of disappearing.

                          After she left, the vision
                          of her nude loomed
upon the silver of the mirror. I walked toward it,
taking off my clothes. That small body
whose desire is not by nature's strict design. My skin
                          smelled like rain, naked. My hair
                          smelled like the black black earth.
Eyes closed, I ran fingers over my clavicle, playing
a silent instrument. On the balcony, a mantis leaped
& became a part of a leaf. I thought of myself
                          spending a whole afternoon staring
                          at a tree, thinking myself a tree.
I thought of the painting, how strokes of desire
poured out of a motionless body perpetually moving;
how loneliness dissected that body
without a galloping thrash. Fear to smash a cello
& find there was no music inside. To admit it was fingers
that made music, it was looking that made beauty.
                        Not me.
                        Not me.
I look into the mirror, as if through my cousin's eyes—
that afternoon, in the rosemary alley, a boy
was kissed by another boy, & both of them tasted of blueberry.

Training

A psychologist told me
we can train our dreams
I practice each night
recite my father's name
and he is a dog
running in and out
of a field of grass
and I the loosened chain
stained with the sweat of his neck

The Boy Is Sleeping

tossed like a winter coat on the couch. Outside
       the frost sheathes telephone poles. I wait

for Zhuangzi's figurative visit in his fugitive cloak.
       He writes me a letter, white syllables

on the nightsilk. I read it in the air: *In the darkness*
       of the north there is a fish, a thousand miles long,

whose name is Vast. It changes into a bird along
       with the autumn water . . . Poor child, your father

named you after a mythcreature, Shangyang, the name
       of a bird, Shangyang, the bird of rain,

whose dance breaks the azure. Poor child, I wish
       you'd never been, were never named after

a rainbird who must unlearn the knowledge of flight
       to survive. I know how you butterfly through rain

into Zhuangzi's dream, asking the Dao of permanence.
       And the answer is *without,* which is now,

you sleeping on the couch, a pure flesh pulseless
       and thin, severed petal, without love or sorrow.

Your green veins throb inside your white collar
       like a bowl of water stirred by light, across

the discrete surface forming a pathway to the without
       of the *without.* I stand in front of you the way

a warm body is insignificant beside its winter coat.

Op. 64 in C♯

to be awake is to find one

-self, raw as a bowl of lilies

waking up in the mirror

Acknowledgment: Erato,

I thank you for permitting bruiseworts lighting my neighbor's yard
    like snow-hooves on the spread plumes
of a blue-naped chlorophonia—no, not a disease but a bird! Thank you
    for twisting ascension in their bones.

Though I cannot fly, in your yawning concession I visit Dublin,
    Hallstatt, Luang Prabang, Beijing, Istanbul
in autumn, Istanbul in spring & O Guanajuato—the flamboyant,

long-legged boys in sea-colored shorts at Jardín de la Unión
    & Kissing Lane chase a cart of key limes
while the vihuela is played & the basilica, the color of Tuscan sun,
    turns velvet in the moon's soft thumb.

    & Kyoto, there a *karesansui* built after the fall
of Edo, the raked white sand in the image of rippling water,
    though I cannot find peace in you, thank you
for cooling a traveler's broken toes. All these places saved me

from my cruel study of a ho-hum self. Though I am becoming
    a total stranger, I thank you for allowing me to keep
these glances on the page, where I see a world distant & undamaged
    by time. Though I cannot stay there, thank you
for favoring my pencil to bear fruits in the vigor of their flesh.

& thank you, Erato, for bringing along with you Daniel,
    who invites me to join his crusade of *inventing*
a new word for green that puts Lorca to shame, who *blasts Schubert*
    in the Whataburger drive-thru & cries on his steering wheel—
O sensitive poets, forgive me for stepping inside your bruise
    that is an open door. Is Johann still *stumbling*
through the transformation of tomatoes while a slice of aurora
    is held in his throat? Our tormenting hours to conjure
words that resist oblivion. Thank you, I would keep that in mind
    for my grocery shopping next time.

Will I ever see you again, Yuki? Are you polishing your nails
        like neon lights in Tokyo? Have your dreams changed—
our vow to become *mist together, bodiless, feeling-less, making our city*
        glisten. Whenever you talk about poetry,
        my heart disintegrates like an origami swan on a stream.

& those moist-eyed gatekeepers on a rotted ladder, my persecutors
washing their brains with newspapers' swart foam, thank you, though
I don't like you. Here, my middle finger is a peace sign of gratitude.

Forgive me, Erato, that in my ardency for poetry, I was not aware
        of the hunger & grief of others.
My apologies for humming the melody of a Mahler symphony
        while the babies on the plane are crying. O off-tuned violins,
        thank you for existing only in Chagall's paintings.

& forgive my obsession with the choreography of trees, my foolish effort
        to empathize with the coldness of a peach, which turns out
to be a grave misunderstanding. O fathomless existence, bear with me
        for peeking into your mystery with the crutches of speech.

Erato, how did you manage to bring Jane from god's nostril—Arizona
        to Austin, to the lake Tahoe of Nevada. Where she cooks
two ill-cooked eggs—blame the altitude!—& a few pieces of dry bread,
        while telling me how Mandelstam begged his neighbor for an egg
        so that Akhmatova would have something to eat
upon her arrival from Leningrad. & upon her arrival in Moscow,
Stalin's troops were already ransacking the apartment, so she asked
Mandelstam to have the egg before the arrest & he did, with some salt.
        On the snow-trooped mountain, I love you & thank you
for the eggs & bread we share—one ache of solitude for two exiles.
While Akhmatova is fumbling *the glove for her left hand onto her right,*
        the sun of yesterday is carried away on a black stretcher.

& thank you, Erato, for pushing me across that broad mahogany
        table of Brigit's, for pushing the glass-sharpened English syllables
out of my mouth onto the page of air, O air of invisible snowy owls

& arctic foxes. Thank you, Brigit, who is now
in the air, for placing my ankles
comfortably inside the wounded openness of poetry.

Please, Erato, let me be humble as I kneel in front of you: my whole body
folds into the bleeding throat of a cuckoo. Quench my ego
the way the midnight street is erased when the headlights of my rented Jeep
are switched off. In exchange, I ask for your indulgence
to whip my words into an atlas of constellations. So that when darkness
comes, when people raise their eyes, the lights
of the universe would meet. The way I was met by the light of others.

Thanks for Reading

Daisies trail the highway, a rock falls and changes the landscape.
I love eating crucian carp and half-cooked eggs. They're sweet.
The scent of raw cilantro. I think mushrooms taste better than some meat.
The textures of fruits are so cold and stiff. I love grapes.
Mincing red poppies with sea salt, I never had it but I think I'll love it.
I like acting, even to myself, only to myself.
I dream a lot, without sleeping. Those dreams damage me.
I rarely talk to my family, and when I do, I feel sorry for myself.
I love my hands.
I care about my face, which is prettier than many.
One night, I dreamt of making love with a woman. It worries me, I think I'm ill.
The other night, with a man. I know I cannot be cured.
I masturbate with my left hand. And write poems with my right hand.
My elbow is my pillow.
Sometimes I wear sneakers that don't match my trousers. No one will notice.
I like to be naked when I'm alone.
My greatest fear is picking up the phone.
The sun-drenched kitchen disappears when I enter my bathroom.
I dislike dreaming while sleeping. I feel powerless in those dreams.
I hurt many people, mostly girls. They deleted me from their phone books.
I miss them in secret.
I was hurt by people, mostly people. I forgive them in order to remember them.
The lotus is at the border of becoming the water, failed by water.
I love flowers, particularly those I cannot name,
as if they have not been given a name.
I love the shape of waves, which is always shaping, yet unshaped
like my mother's hair, once braided by my father's hands, unbraided, by time.
Each water bottle is a small buddha
that invites light to pierce its boneless musing.
The necklace that the sunset left on the terra-cotta roof is semisweet.
The water is comfortable in the bottle as much as it would be in a pond.
I prefer pencils not to fall from the table.
Staplers, shoes, lampposts, I think whatever is not moving is waiting.
I like the idea that everything could be poetic, especially my being poetic.

I dislike the idea that everything *is* about power.
I don't argue against it, just dislike it.
Once I passed by a bakery selling croissants made of moonbeams.
I was happy. The moon must taste of flour and butter.
Once at a square in Marseille, all pedestrians were stopped by an oboe player.
Once a man, near the windowpane, felt an incessant pain and he was sad
for nothing he could be sad about.
Goodbye, goodbye, I'm going to write at the seaside.
Once the words were meant to lie and we relied on them to live.

Displaced Distance as a Red Berry

Inkstone is there. Unfolded envelope is there.
Kitchen is there, drenched with the smell of chicken soup.
Red berry is there, so is the lovesickness it causes.
Luna moths are there. They mistake the lantern for a palanquin.
Evening-old chrysanthemums are there, tossing their lion-shaped faces,
      untainted by brutality.
Akhmatova's missing hero is there, somewhere
      bargaining with a taxi driver, "Fifty rubles to Leningrad."
Married martyr is there, cupping a cloud of hydrangeas
      as a hydrogen bomb, so the mortals in the bar stay far from him.
Loquat is there, its succulence the enactment of the season.
Tomas Tranströmer is there, though he claims *I'm not here*
      he is there. He is there, where *waking up is a parachute jump*
      from dreams, where the grass is greener than the color of grass.
Lovers are touching not talking by a lake. Soon they will just be friends.
Poets are dreaming not writing, so are the beetles in the lazy air.
Princess is there, whose lilac hands rinse the reflection of moon
      bestrewn like a dress for the princess's
      stepmother, whose body is a dagger.
Stepmother is there, enticing my father with her breastbone.
Father is chasing after her symphonic hair like a long note, a fermata
      in Chopin's piano sonata. Chopin is sick and unnoticed,
      playing his heroic ballade only as the background music.
Red berries, according to Chinese legend,
      are the blood-tears of a wife, whose husband died in a war.
War is there, each pale soldier with torn limb an Icarus,
      each hospital a white dream, and each body smoothed
      like a wing, not of an angel but of a flying animal.
Angels, though today they're just winged animals, are there.
Red berries are there. That is why I am writing you this letter.
      Rain, and the stairs are washed white.
      Windows opened, so the wind might be present.
      Dark noise of cars is there, people leaving somewhere
      for somewhere else, which they will leave again.

I imagine when you read this letter my rain will not wet
       your socks, my mind will not flutter your collar.
       I won't be here, where curtains shift like sea
       without me, where lamplight shines for nobody.
Stars are there, unnamed. We give them names knowing
       they will never turn back for our calling.
Cat-furred lamplight is there, laced with the ice-feathered
       moonlight, making here more desolate.
Bed is there. I'll only sleep on the left side, where you once slept,
       leaving the right empty, pretending
       I am not there.
But whatever is not there is there in red berries,
       in the widow's bloodred tears, strewn for the missing—you
       are here—more real than the lamp and ink and moonlight,
       the way I am there—home, late from work, soaked in rain.
There—tell me to stop writing this letter, hand me the armful
of chrysanthemums you've been picking for the whole afternoon.

Acknowledgments

Early versions of some poems have appeared in *AGNI, BOAAT Journal, Colorado Review, Epiphany, The Georgia Review, Guernica, Gulf Coast, Hobart, The Iowa Review, jubilat, Narrative, The Nation, New England Review, Ninth Letter, Omnium Gatherum Quarterly, Ploughshares, The Shanghai Literary Review, Southword, TriQuarterly, Washington Square Review, The Yale Review, Truth to Power: Writers Respond to the Rhetoric of Hate and Fear,* and *The Forward Book of Poetry 2020.* The epigraph and section titles use lines from "Deep Winter" by Du Fu. The title *"Easier to Lift a Stone Than to Say Your Name"* borrows a line from Osip Mandelstam, and *"Time the Stone Makes an Effort to Flower"* from Paul Celan. Deep gratitude to my teachers and mentors, who have faith in this young poet writing in a strange language: Brigit Pegeen Kelly, Janice N. Harrington, Joy Harjo, Michael Madonick, Henri Cole, Dean Young, Carrie Fountain, Lisa Olstein, Roger Reeves, Joanna Klink, Paisley Rekdal, Patrick Phillips, and the forever and only Jane Miller. Thank you all for breathing poetry into my soul. Thanks to Forrest Gander and Robert Hass, who helped make this dream project a reality, and to Louise Glück who at the last minute transformed it. To my fellow Stegners at Stanford University for their unyielding support. I have benefited from your startling brilliance. For my dearest friends who hold my hands through the darkest hours: Liyuan Yin, Min Zhang, Fangdai Chen, Lianghao Cao, Daniel Ruiz, Johann Sarna, Suphil Lee Park, Yuki Tanaka, Tracey Rose Peyton, and Rachel Heng. Without any of you, this book would be impossible. I am deeply indebted to my editor Michael Wiegers and the fantastic team at Copper Canyon Press. Thanks to Michener Center for Writers, Munster Literature Centre, Community of Writers, Vermont Studio Center, and the Creative Writing Program at Stanford University for offering me the lavish time and space to complete this collection. And thank you, Muses, whatever names or forms you take, for guiding me into poetry, for granting me a second life.

About the Author

Shangyang Fang comes from Chengdu, China. His eponym, Shangyang, was a mythological one-legged bird whose dance brought forth rain and flood.

Lannan Literary Selections

For two decades Lannan Foundation has supported the publication and distribution of exceptional literary works. Copper Canyon Press gratefully acknowledges their support.

LANNAN LITERARY SELECTIONS 2021

Shangyang Fang, *Burying the Mountain*

June Jordan, *The Essential June Jordan*

Laura Kasischke, *Lightning Falls in Love*

Arthur Sze, *The Glass Constellation: New and Collected Poems*

Fernando Valverde (translated by Carolyn Forché), *América*

RECENT LANNAN LITERARY SELECTIONS FROM COPPER CANYON PRESS

Mark Bibbins, *13th Balloon*

Sherwin Bitsui, *Dissolve*

Jericho Brown, *The Tradition*

Victoria Chang, *Obit*

Leila Chatti, *Deluge*

John Freeman, *Maps*

Jenny George, *The Dream of Reason*

Deborah Landau, *Soft Targets*

Rachel McKibbens, *blud*

Philip Metres, *Shrapnel Maps*

Aimee Nezhukumatathil, *Oceanic*

Camille Rankine, *Incorrect Merciful Impulses*

Paisley Rekdal, *Nightingale*

Natalie Scenters-Zapico, *Lima :: Limón*

Natalie Shapero, *Popular Longing*

Frank Stanford, *What About This: Collected Poems of Frank Stanford*

C.D. Wright, *Casting Deep Shade*

Matthew Zapruder, *Father's Day*

Poetry is vital to language and living. Since 1972, Copper Canyon Press has published extraordinary poetry from around the world to engage the imaginations and intellects of readers, writers, booksellers, librarians, teachers, students, and donors.

Copper Canyon Press gratefully acknowledges the kindness, patronage, and generous support of Jean Marie Lee, whose love and passionate appreciation of poetry has provided an everlasting benefit to our publishing program.

WE ARE GRATEFUL FOR THE MAJOR SUPPORT PROVIDED BY:

THE PAUL G. ALLEN
FAMILY FOUNDATION

The Chinese character for poetry is made up of two parts:
"word" and "temple." It also serves as pressmark for
Copper Canyon Press.

The poems are set in Fournier.
Book design and composition by Phil Kovacevich.